All A[illegible]
Soccer

by Michèle Dufresne

Pioneer Valley Educational Press, Inc.

Soccer is a fun sport.

Many people like to play soccer.

Soccer is a team sport.
There are 11 players
on a team.

The players work together to score
goals for their team.

Players kick the ball
with their feet. They can
also use their body
or their head.

The players can’t use
their arms or hands to catch
or throw the ball.

To score, soccer players kick the ball to the other team's **goal**. When they kick the ball into the net, they score one point for their team.

The **goalie** will try to keep the other team from kicking the ball into the net. Only the goalies can use their hands or arms to catch the ball.

In soccer, it is good
to work together to score.
A good soccer player
will kick the ball
to another player on his or her team.
This can help keep
the other team
from getting the ball.

Breaking a rule is called a **foul**. A player cannot kick, push, or trip another player. Players cannot touch the ball with their hands.

If a player breaks a rule, the other team gets a free kick.

8

If the ball is high in the air, a player can use his or her head to hit the ball. This is called a **header**.

Soccer is a fast sport.
Players have to run up and down the field with the ball.
Soccer players need to be fast!

GLOSSARY

foul: when a player breaks the rules of the game

goal: the net that players kick the ball into to score points

goalie: the player who guards the goal and tries to stop the other team from scoring

header: when a player hits a soccer ball with his or her head